Vocabulary Booster
for Cambridge English Qualifications

PRE A1 STARTERS

How to use this book

Introduction

Team Together Vocabulary Boosters are designed to be a fun and engaging way of consolidating and extending vocabulary from the *Team Together* series. Each Vocabulary Booster includes 10 units, based around a different topic relevant to children and their lives. The books also offer support for children preparing for the Cambridge English Qualifications for young learners.

Vocabulary presentation

In the first part of each unit, key vocabulary is introduced in the context of a large, colourful scene, which will engage children and spark their curiosity. Children are encouraged to explore the scene through a series of short activities and accompanying audio.

Labels for key vocabulary.

Blank labels add an extra level of challenge for stronger students.

Audio and exercises present the language in context.

Fun facts boxes give children additional information about the topic. Remember! boxes give tips on language, e.g. Irregular English spelling patterns.

Additional questions encourage children to explore the scene further.

Children find Ronny the rabbit hiding in each scene.

Vocabulary practice

In the second part of each unit, there are two pages of activities which provide further consolidation and practice of the vocabulary through a variety of fun activities.

Target icons identify Cambridge English Qualifications style tasks.

Vocabulary practised through reading and listening tasks.

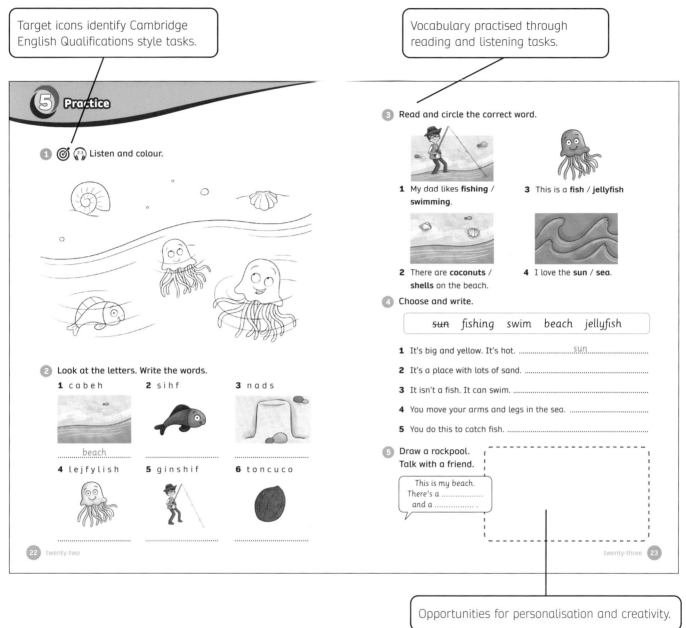

Opportunities for personalisation and creativity.

Other books in the series

There are three Vocabulary Booster books in the *Team Together* series, each one relating to one of the Cambridge English Qualifications for young learners tests:

- Pre A1 Starters
- A1 Movers
- A2 Flyers

We suggest that you use the Vocabulary Booster for Cambridge English Qualifications Pre A1 Starters with *Team Together* Levels 1 and 2.

Our final tip for using this book? Have fun!

1 Numbers and colours

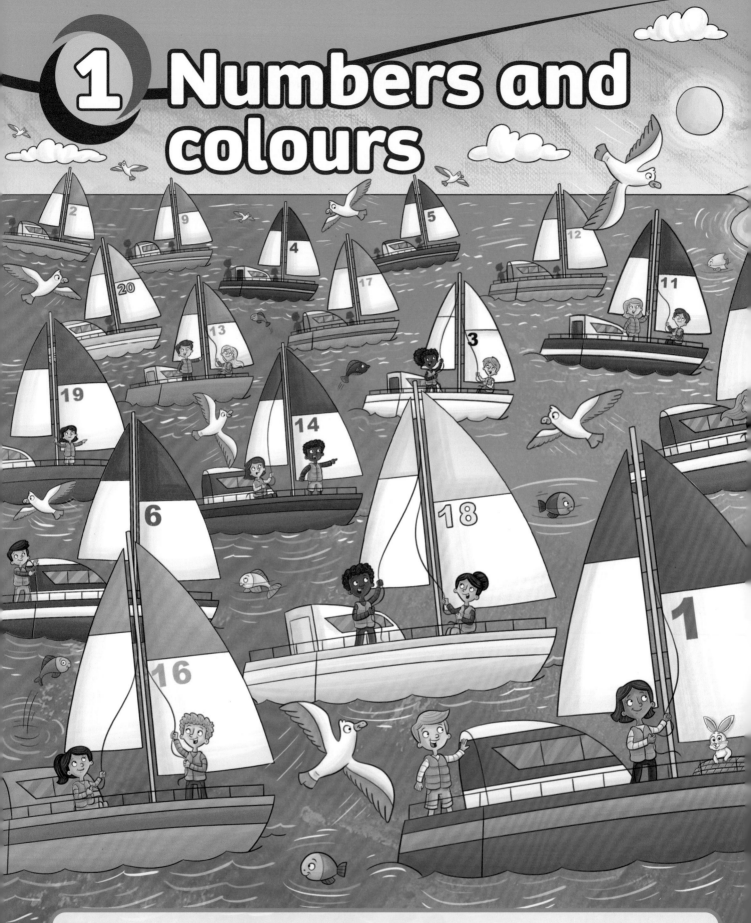

Colours

	red	orange	brown
grey	green	pink	black
blue	yellow	purple	white

1 (1.1) Listen and point. Repeat the numbers.

2 (1.2) Listen and say the chant.

3 (1.3) Listen and say the colours.

4 How many ... can you see?

1 grey boats ☐

2 blue boats ☐

3 green boats ☐

4 orange boats ☐

5 What colour is boat ... ?

12 ....   6 ....

7 ....   9 ....

Where's Ronny?

Fun fact
Yellow and blue make green. What colour do blue and red make?

Numbers

1 one	**11** eleven
2 two	**12** twelve
3 three	**13** thirteen
4 four	**14** fourteen
5 five	**15** fifteen
6 six	**16** sixteen
7 seven	**17** seventeen
8 eight	**18** eighteen
9 nine	**19** nineteen
10 ten	**20** twenty

1 Write the words and numbers.

2 Count and circle.

1 eighteen / sixteen

2 thirteen / eleven

3 fifteen / fourteen

4 twenty / twelve

3 Look and colour.

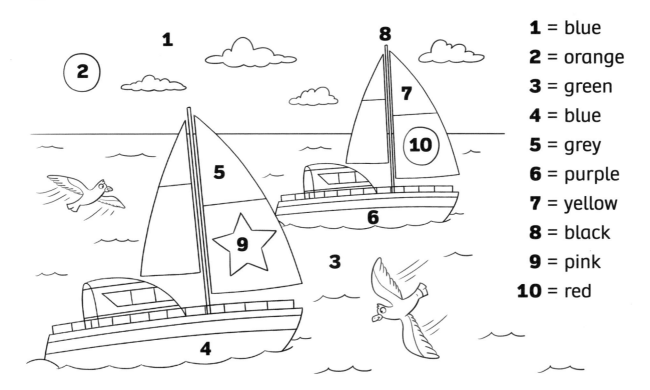

1 = blue
2 = orange
3 = green
4 = blue
5 = grey
6 = purple
7 = yellow
8 = black
9 = pink
10 = red

4 Complete the sentences.

1 It's red.

2 It's ....

3 It's ....

4 It's ....

5 It's ....

6 It's ....

5 Draw and colour your boat.

My boat is
....

2 My school

keyboard

drawing

draw

painting

1

2

3

board

class

4

paper

mouse

tablet

classmate

1 (2.1) Listen and point.
Repeat the words.

2 (2.2) Listen and circle.

3 What colour ...
1 is the tablet? ....
2 are the desks? ....
3 is the mouse? ....
4 are the chairs? ....

4 Look and find. What is it?

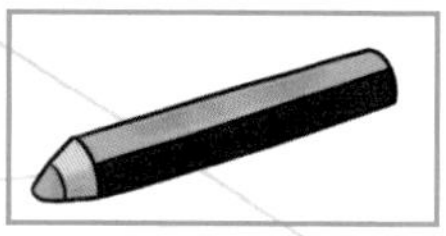

Fun fact

= mouse   = mouse

Where's Ronny?

1 Follow and write.

1

2

3

4

5

6

k e y b o a r d

c _ _ _ _ _

d _ _ _ _ _ _

m _ _ _ _

p _ _ _ _ _ _ _

p _ _ _ _

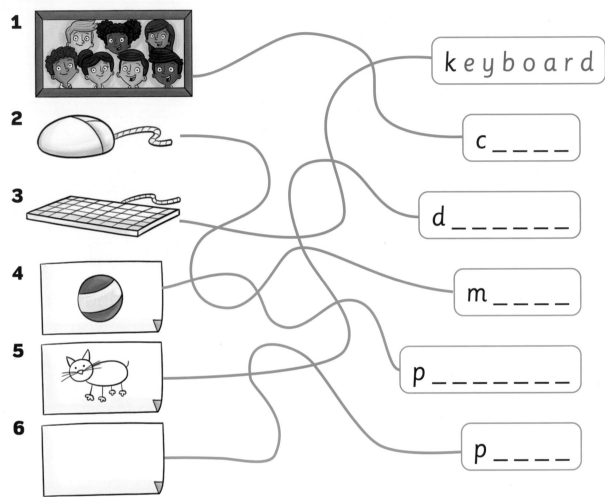

2 (2.3) Listen and number.

a

b   1

c

d

3 Read and circle.

1 This is my **tablet / mouse**.

3 We're **classmates / class**.

2 Look at the **paper / board**.

4 I can **paint / draw**.

4 Join the dots. Write the words.

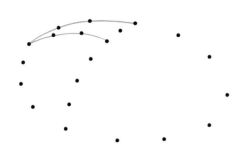

This is a ……………………………… .

This is a ……………………………… .

5 Draw something in your classroom.

This is my drawing. It's a ……………… .

3 My toys

teddy

helicopter

boy

1

lorry

train

alien

plane

monster

girl

robot

2

1 🎧 3.1 Listen and point.
Repeat the words.

2 🎧 3.2 Listen and say the chant.

3 Count.
How many .... are there?
  1 robots ☐
  2 aliens ☐
  3 monsters ☐
  4 planes ☐

4 What colour is the lorry?

....

Remember!

lorry   truck

Where's Ronny?

1 (3.3) **Listen and tick.**

1 What's Ben's favourite toy?

a

b

c

2 What toy has Mia got?

a

b

c

3 Who's got a teddy?

a

b

c

2 **Write the missing letters. Then match.**

1 l_o_rry

2 p_ane

3 mons_er

4 rob_t

5 tedd_

6 trai_

3 Read and colour the toys.

1 The lorry is **red**.

2 The alien is **purple**.

3 The monster is **green**.

4 The plane is **pink**.

5 The helicopter is **yellow**.

6 The train is **blue**.

4 Trace. Then write.

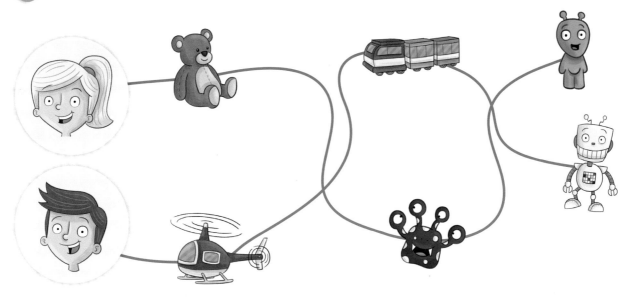

1 The girl's got a .... , a .... and an ....

2 The boy's got a .... , a .... and a ....

5 Now draw.

This is my
....

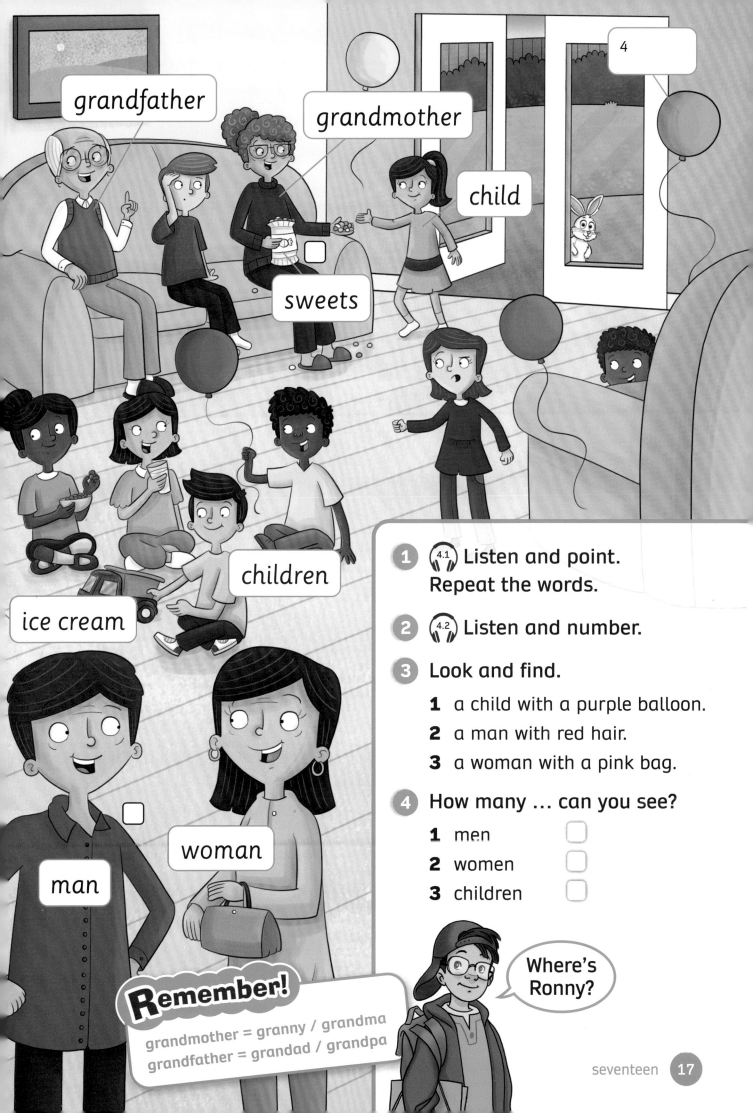

grandfather

grandmother

child

4

sweets

children

ice cream

man

woman

1 (4.1) **Listen and point. Repeat the words.**

2 (4.2) **Listen and number.**

3 **Look and find.**

1 a child with a purple balloon.

2 a man with red hair.

3 a woman with a pink bag.

4 **How many ... can you see?**

1 men ☐

2 women ☐

3 children ☐

Where's Ronny?

Remember!
grandmother = granny / grandma
grandfather = grandad / grandpa

1 🎯 🎧 (4.3) Listen and draw lines.

| Charlie | Jim | Julia | Daisy | Zoe |

2 Find and write.

1 man

2 ....

3 ....

4 ....

5 ....

6 ....

7 ....

8 ....

3 Read and write *Yes* or *No*.

1 The child has got sweets. ....Yes....

2 The women have got lemonade. ....

3 The man has got cake. ....

4 The children have got ice cream. ....

4 Choose and write.

> children   women   grandmother   ~~man~~
> child   woman   grandfather   men

1 This ......*man*...... is my dad. These .... are my uncles.
2 This .... is my mum. These .... are my aunts.
3 This .... is my baby brother. These .... are my friends.
4 The man with grey hair is my ....
5 The woman with grey hair is my ....

5 Draw your family.
Talk with a friend.

> This is my family.
> This is my ....

5 At the beach

coconut

fishing

beach

sea

jellyfish

fish

sun

shell

sand

swim

1 Listen and point. Repeat the words.

2 Listen and say the chant.

3 Look and circle.

1 a blue fish
2 a white shell
3 a red ball
4 a brown coconut

4 How many balls can you see?

Fun fact

Jellyfish aren't fish! They can be pink, yellow, purple or blue!

Where's Ronny?

5 **Practice**

1 🎯 🎧 (2.3) Listen and colour.

2 Look at the letters. Write the words.

1 c a b e h

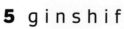
beach
....

2 s i h f

....

3 n a d s

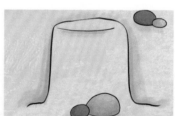

....

4 l e j f y l i s h

....

5 g i n s h i f

....

6 t o n c u c o

....

3 Read and circle the correct word.

1 My dad likes **fishing** / **swimming**.

2 There are **coconuts** / **shells** on the beach.

3 This is a **fish** / **jellyfish**

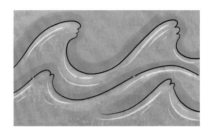

4 I love the **sun** / **sea**.

4 Choose and write.

> ~~sun~~   *fishing*   swim   beach   jellyfish

1 It's big and yellow. It's hot. .... *sun* ....

2 It's a place with lots of sand. ....

3 It isn't a fish. It can swim. ....

4 You move your arms and legs in the sea. ....

5 You do this to catch fish. ....

5 Draw a rockpool.
Talk with a friend.

> This is my beach.
> There's a ....
> and a ....

Review 1

1 **Read and colour.**

1 nine

2 twelve

3 fifteen

4 eighteen

2 **Read and write *Yes* or *No*.**

1
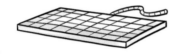
It's a keyboard. ...Yes...

2
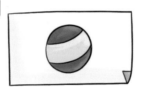
It's a drawing. ....

3

They're classmates. ....

4

It's a tablet. ....

5

It's a mouse. ....

6

It's a painting. ....

3 **Look and write the toy words.**

1 The ...teddy... is **brown**.

2 The .... is **grey**.

3 The .... is **green**.

4 The .... is **purple**.

5 The .... is **blue**.

6 The .... is **yellow**.

4 🎧 (R1.1) **Listen and tick.**

1

a ☐

b ☐

2

a ☐

b ☐

3

a ☐

b ☐

4

a ☐

b ☐

5 **Count and write.**

In the picture there are ...

three ....jellyfish....

four ....

five ....

eleven ....

bathroom

bath

kitchen

dining room

radio

chips

mat

pie

1

2

living room

watch

3

4

1 🎧 **6.1 Listen and point. Repeat the words.**

2 🎧 **6.2 Listen and say the room.**

3 **Where's the … ?**

cow ....

mouse ....

cat ....

spider ....

4 **How many … are there in the dining room?**

1 men ☐

2 women ☐

3 children ☐

Where's Ronny?

Remember!

chips

fries

twenty-seven **27**

6 Practice

1 Find and circle.

1

2

3

b	a	r	m	a	t
a	n	a	x	p	z
t	q	d	p	c	w
h	w	i	i	m	a
b	u	o	e	r	t
x	z	p	h	f	c
c	h	i	p	s	h

4

5

6

2 Write the room words.

1 .... *bedroom* ....

2 ....

3 ....

4 ....

5 ....

3  **Listen and draw.**

4 **Look at activity 3. Complete the sentences.**
Then ask and answer.

1 There's a .... TV .... in the .... living room ....

2 There's a .... in the ....

3 There's a .... in the ....

4 There's a .... in the ....

5 There's a .... in the ....

6 There's some .... in the ....

(Where's the radio?) (It's in the bedroom.)

5 **Draw your home and write.**

I watch TV in the

....

I sleep in my

....

I eat in the

....

7 At the market

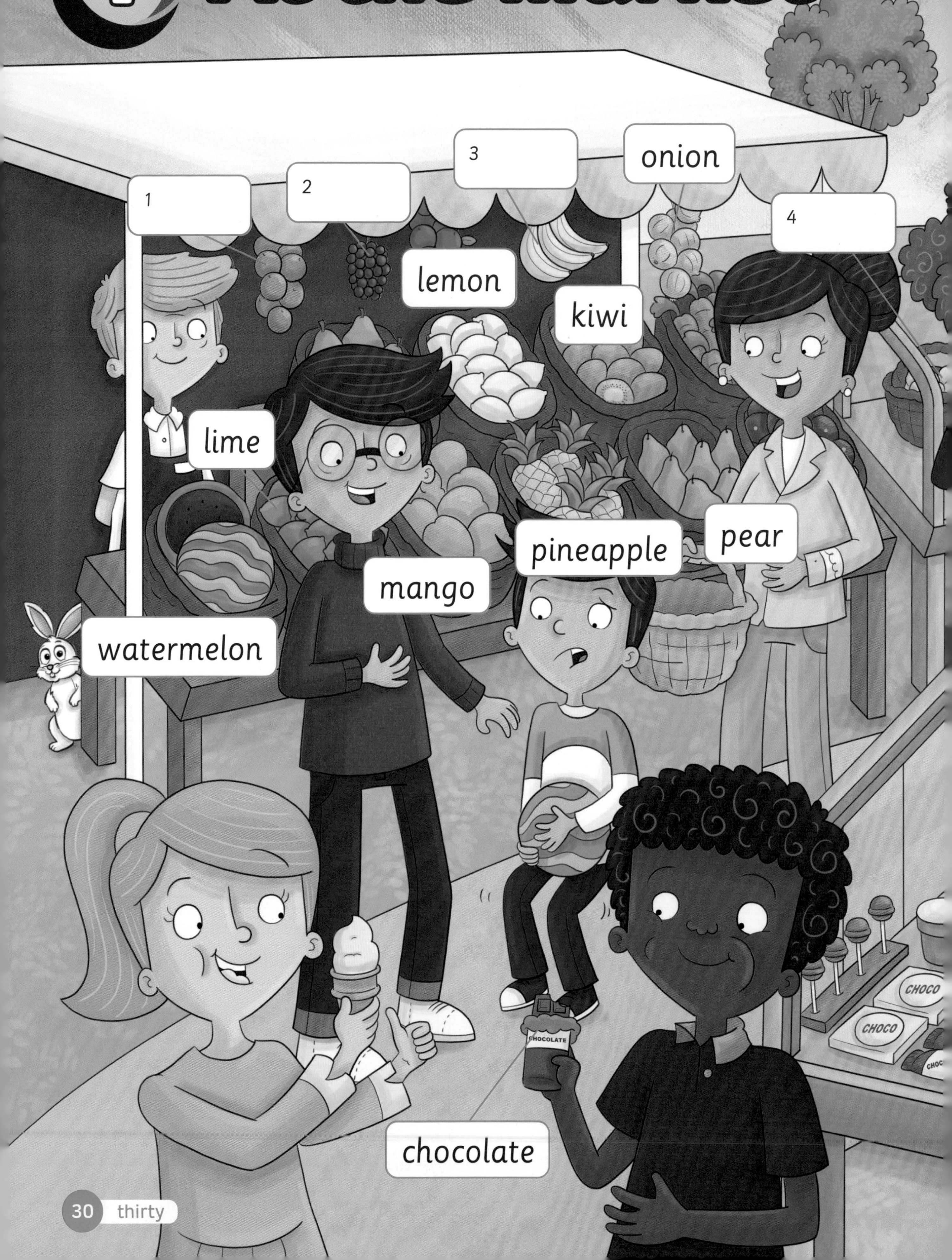
1
2
3
onion
4
lemon
kiwi
lime
pineapple
pear
mango
watermelon
CHOCOLATE
CHOCO
CHOCO
chocolate

5

6

8

meatballs

7

1 🎧 **Listen and point. Repeat the words.**

2 🎧 **Listen and say the chant.**

3 **How many ... are there?**

1 lemons ☐
2 watermelons ☐
3 pineapples ☐
4 pears ☐

4 **How many other foods can you find in the picture?**

Where's Ronny?

Remember!

one mango → two mangoes
one potato → two potatoes
one tomato → two tomatoes

1 a) Circle the words. Then write.

pear watermelon lemon onion mango pineapple lime

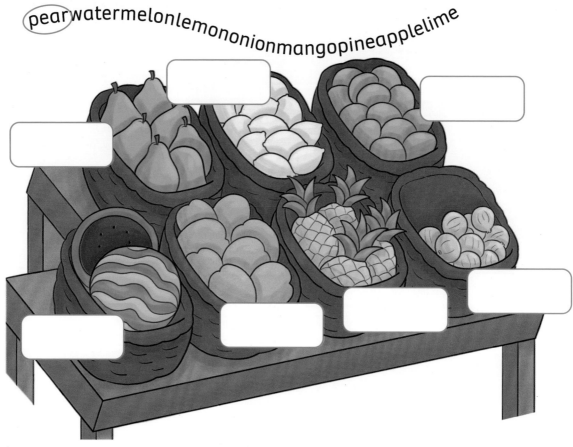

b) Which food is different? ....

2 🎧 (7.3) Listen and tick.

1   a   b

2   a   b

3 **Read and write the words.**

> kiwis   pineapple   meatballs   ~~onions~~
> chocolate   mangoes

1 Hello. Can I help you?

Yes, can I have some [1] .... onions .... please?

And some [2] ....

What about some [3] .... ?

No, I don't like kiwis.

2 Can I have some [4] .... please?

And a [5] ....

What about some [6] .... ?

Oh, yes please!

4 **Write. Then tell a friend.**

1 I like ...

....
....
....
....

2 I don't like ...

....
....
....
....

5 **Draw your favourite food. Then write.**

My favourite food is
....

8 Sports day

basketball

hit

1

bounce

hockey

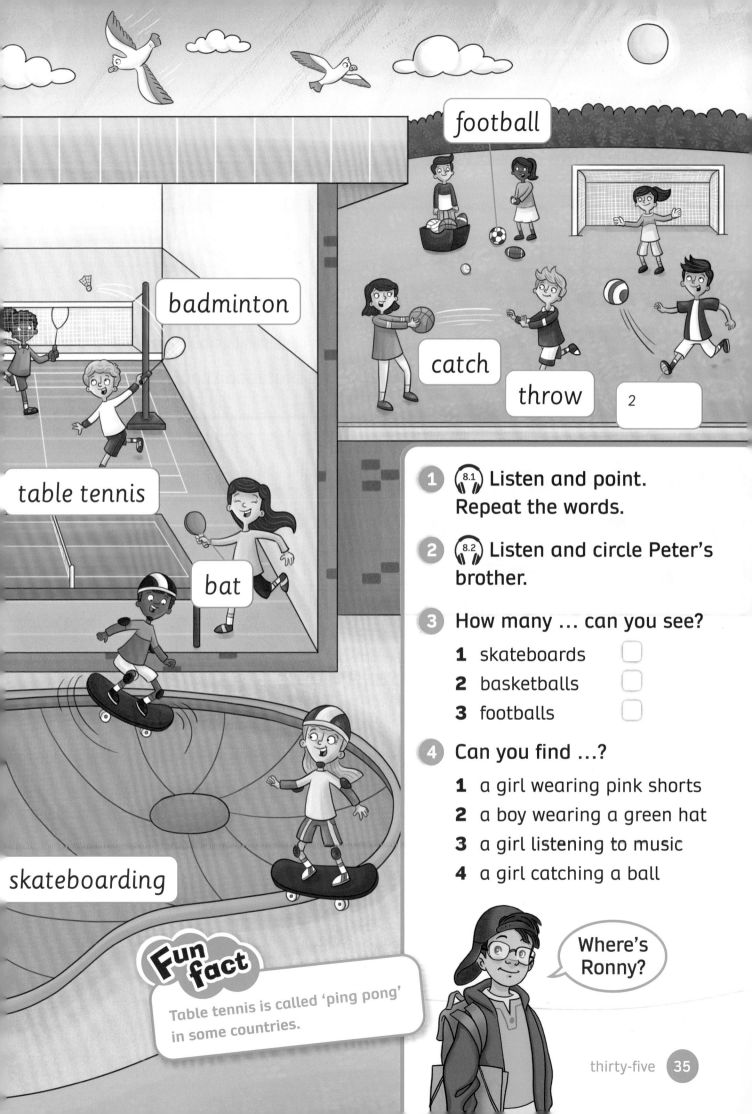

football

badminton

catch

throw

2

table tennis

bat

skateboarding

Fun fact
Table tennis is called 'ping pong' in some countries.

1 🎧 8.1 **Listen and point. Repeat the words.**

2 🎧 8.2 **Listen and circle Peter's brother.**

3 **How many … can you see?**

    1 skateboards ☐

    2 basketballs ☐

    3 footballs ☐

4 **Can you find …?**

    1 a girl wearing pink shorts

    2 a boy wearing a green hat

    3 a girl listening to music

    4 a girl catching a ball

Where's Ronny?

1 Circle the correct word.

basketball / table tennis

skateboarding / hockey

tennis / badminton

throw / catch

2 🎯 🎧 (8.3) Listen and number.

3 Look and write *Yes* or *No*.

1 The children are playing hockey. ......No......

2 They're playing table tennis. ....

3 They've got bats. ....

4 They've got skateboards. ....

5 They're catching and throwing the ball. ....

6 They're hitting the ball with their bats. ....

4 Now choose and write.

| bats | basketball | hitting | ~~ball~~ | bouncing |

They've got an orange ¹......ball...... .

They haven't got ²............................ .

The girl is ³............................ the ball.

She isn't ⁴............................ the ball.

They're playing ⁵............................ .

5 Draw a sport you like. Write a description.

> I like
> ....

9 At the zoo

monkey

flower

polar bear

elephant

hippo

giraffe

zebra

camera

tree

bear

1 (9.1) Listen and point.
Repeat the words.

2 (9.2) Listen and say the chant.

3 Can you find ...?
1 a black and white animal ☐
2 a grey animal ☐
3 a tall animal ☐
4 an animal with a long tail ☐
5 a purple flower ☐

4 Now close your book.
How many different animals
can you remember?

Where's Ronny?

Fun fact
Polar bears like swimming. They're fast. They can swim at 10km/hour!

1 🎯 **Write the words.**

1 fragife

 ...g i r a f f e...

2 eret

 ....

3 lopra aber

 ....

4 palethen

 ....

5 amarec

 ....

6 wolfer

 ....

2 **Look and write *Yes* or *No*.**

Is it a hippo? ....

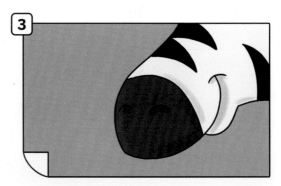

Is it a polar bear? ....

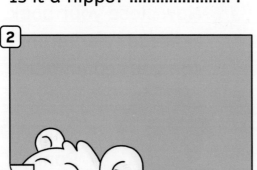

Is it a giraffe? ....

Is it a monkey? ....

3 Read and match.

1 It's big and grey. It's got big ears.
2 It lives in the snow. It likes fish. It's white.
3 It's yellow and brown. It's got long legs.
4 It's brown. It can climb trees. It likes fruit.

It's a polar bear.

It's a bear.

It's a giraffe.

It's an elephant.

4 Read and write the words.

flower   camera   trees   monkeys   ~~zoo~~

This is me and my friend Sally. We're at the ¹......ZOO...... .
I've got my ².................. .
I'm taking a photo of the ³................ . They're small and brown.
They can jump and swing in the ⁴................ .
Look, that monkey has got a ⁵...................... !

5 Draw an animal at the zoo. Then write.

This is a ....
It's got ....
It can ....

10 In the city

park

3

4

5

6

1 🎧 10.1 **Listen and point. Repeat the words.**

2 🎧 10.2 **Listen. What city words do you hear?**

3 **Find and circle.**

1 a yellow lorry.
2 a red helicopter.
3 a green bus.

4 a woman driving a pink car.
5 a boy riding an orange bike.
6 a yellow helicopter.

4 **Count. How many ... can you see?**

1 cars ☐
2 ships ☐
3 buses ☐
4 trains ☐
5 lorries ☐

Where's Ronny?

Remember!

drive → driving
ride → riding

1 Find and circle the words. Then write.

1 ....bus........

c	v	t	y	b	o	m	s
l	b	u	s	i	m	n	h
o	g	h	s	k	z	x	o
s	d	d	w	e	h	s	p
e	l	o	r	r	y	h	j
d	s	c	v	b	i	i	k
z	d	r	i	v	e	p	f
p	a	r	k	n	c	v	x

5 ....

2 ....

6 ....

3 ....

7 ....

4 ....

8 ....

2 Match the words to the verbs.

lorry car plane
bike helicopter
horse train **kite**

ride

drive

fly

3 🎯 🎧(10.3) **Listen and tick.**

1 How does Jim go to school?

a  ☐

b  ☐

c  ☐

2 Where do Charlie and Lily go?

a 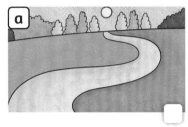 ☐

b  ☐

c  ☐

3 What's Sally's favourite way to travel?

a 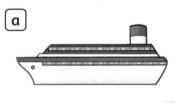 ☐

b  ☐

c  ☐

4 **Read and write the words.**

1 A: Can you .... a car?

B: No, but I can .... a bike.

| ride drive fly |

2 A: Can you fly a .... ?

B: No, but I can .... a plane.

| ride helicopter fly |

3 A: Is the .... open?

B: No, it's ....

| closed train shop |

5 **Draw. How do you like to travel?**

I like

....

Review 2

1 (R2.1) **Listen and match.**

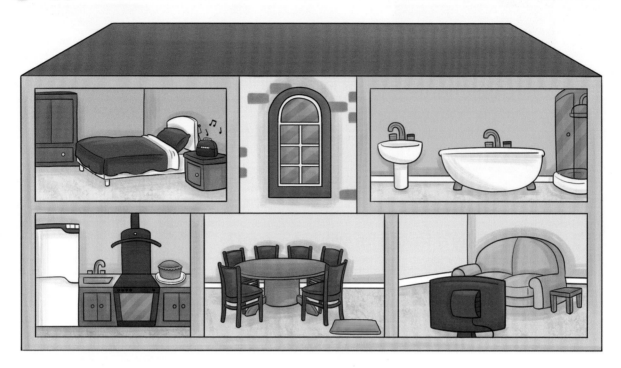

2 **Match the words.**

carrot   meatballs   watermelon   lime   onion   pineapple

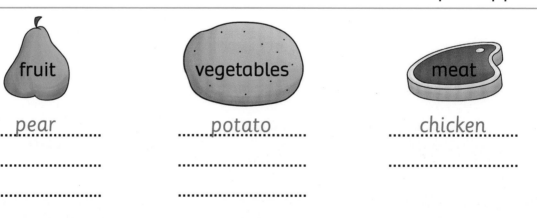

fruit   vegetables   meat

...........pear...........   ....potato...........   ....chicken...........

....

....

....

3 **Read and match.**

1 You run and hit the ball. ....hockey.......

2 You hit the ball with a small bat. ....

3 You run, jump and bounce a ball. ....

4 You jump on a board. ....

4 Complete the crossword.

Across

4 6

Down

1

2

3

5

5 Read and tick or cross.

1

The shop is open. ✓

2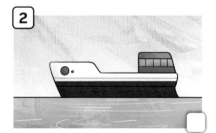

It's a big lorry.

3

She can drive a car.

4

This is a plane.

5

He can ride a bus.

6

The shop is closed.

Extra vocabulary

1 (EV1) **Listen, point and say.**

| day | morning | evening | night |

2 (EV2) (EV3) **Listen and repeat. Then listen and number.**

in   on   under

behind   in front of   between

3 (EV4) (EV5) **Listen and repeat. Then listen and circle.**

1    **2**    **3**    **4**

beautiful   young   tall   scary

ugly   old   short   funny